Gingersnaps

Daily Affirmations
for African American Children
and Families

Anita Alexander and Susan Payne
Illustrated by Nancy Doniger

Jump at the Sun
Hyperion Books for Children
New York

First Edition
1 3 5 7 9 10 8 6 4 2
Printed in the United States of America.

Designed by Stephanie Bart-Horvath.
This book is set in 14-point Tiepolo Book.
Library of Congress Cataloging-in-Publication Data
has been applied for.
ISBN 0-7868-1306-7

This book is dedicated to our children,
Alexandria and Avery,
Ashley Kathleen and Courtney Elisabeth.

We would like to thank our literary agent,
Marie Brown, and our editor, Andrea Davis Pinkney. We
would also like to thank the following people for their love
and support: Homer and Naomi Pierce, Walter, Jean and
Kathy Alexander, Daphne Muse, Diana Marie,
Stephanie India, Lionel Seals, and Paul Payne.

— A. A. & S. P.

Introduction

Gingersnaps is a gift to you—a gift to show you just how truly special you are. As an African American, you are not only unique, but also intelligent, strong, and very beautiful. This book of affirmations is to remind you of the power you have within you. This power gives you the freedom to make choices in your life—choices about who you are and what you want to be. Like yourself just as you are. You are

perfect! You are wonderful! • Imagine this book as a mother's warm hug to help you through your day. Read an affirmation each day to remind yourself that you can choose how you feel and how you act. Your thoughts are powerful. So, think good, happy, peaceful thoughts. Think about things that make you smile and fill you with joy. You'll soon find out that when you feel good, you *do* good. And with a positive spirit and a winning attitude, you can achieve any level of greatness that you desire. • Ask your parents to join you in your daily readings. Together you can read each affirmation and discuss any questions or ideas that you might have. At the end of the day you can talk about how the affirmation made you feel. Did it help you with a problem? Did it make you feel good about yourself or change a bad mood? • As a child, you are God's gift to the world; we give thanks for each and every one of you. Know that you are loved and cherished.

Always,
ANITA ALEXANDER & SUSAN PAYNE

January

JUST ABOUT ME

*E*very day I am growing and learning new things about the world I live in and the people around me. Most of all, I am learning new things about myself— what I can do and what I can be. • I know that what I think about myself is important, because if I feel good about myself, there's nothing that I can't achieve. So, sometimes I like to remind myself of all the things that make me special, like my bright eyes and wonderful smile, or my confidence and curiosity about everything. • It was her confidence in herself and her curiosity about the world that led Mae C. Jemison to dream of traveling in space. As a child, she loved to read, learn, and explore, and she decided that nothing would stop her from becoming an astronaut. In college Mae earned degrees in science, Afro-American studies, and medicine. • In 1992, after many years of studying and never giving up on her dream, Mae C. Jemison became the first African American female astronaut. This month I'll think about the kind of person that I am now, and what my dreams are for my future. I'm going to spend some time thinking just about me.

J ANUARY 1

Hooray for this brand-new year!
Today is the day I celebrate myself.

JANUARY 2

When I look in the mirror, I am
bright and beautiful, one of a kind,
and absolutely wonderful.

JANUARY 3

Today I will write down four good
things I like about myself. Thank
you, God, for making me special.

J A N U A R Y   4

Long or short, Afro or locks,
shaved or buzzed, my hair is just
perfect for me.

J A N U A R Y   5

My name is special. I say my name
out loud—how sweet the sound.

JANUARY 6

There is not a single person in this world like me. That's pretty cool.

JANUARY 7

I am a work of art—designed and created by God.

JANUARY 8

Today I will spend a little quiet time alone. I'll think about all my favorite things. I'm getting to know me.

JANUARY 9

Guess what I like best? I like me.

JANUARY 10

Today I will eat foods that are
good for me. I'll get plenty of rest.
I am taking care of myself.

JANUARY 11

I know when to shout, when to
whisper, and when to be quiet.
I think before I speak.

JANUARY 12

I let the way I act, look, and talk
tell others how I feel about myself.

JANUARY 13

I am a precious jewel, to be loved
and treasured.

JANUARY 14

My body's shape and size are all
right with me.

JANUARY 15

When I walk, I stand tall. My head
is up, my shoulders are back. I am
proud to be me.

JANUARY 16

I love my beautiful brown self.

JANUARY 17

When I talk, I speak slowly. I
speak clearly. I am making myself
understood.

JANUARY 18

I am a leader, not a follower.

JANUARY 19

When I put my mind to it, I
can *do* anything. I can *be*
anything.

JANUARY 20

My best friend is me. I am never
alone.

JANUARY 21

Hey! I am not my mother, father, brother, or sister. I am me.

JANUARY 22

Today I am happy and thankful for everything I have.

JANUARY 23

I love every little bit of me.

JANUARY 24
I am smart, beautiful, different,
and totally fabulous.

JANUARY 25
My good manners make me nice to
know.

JANUARY 26
I love the skin I'm in. It covers me
from head to toe in beautiful
shades of brown.

JANUARY 27

I'm careful about what I say about myself and others.

JANUARY 28

Today I am going to think of all the things that make me an original.

JANUARY 29

I am a bright and shining star.

JANUARY 30

God created the heavens and Earth and everything in them. I am a magnificent creation of God!

JANUARY 31

Rainbows, snowflakes, butterflies, and me. Oh, what a miracle I am.

February

HERITAGE

My heritage has been passed down to me from my ancestors. Heritage is the history of my people, showing up in the way I look, think, speak, and act. It's the color of my skin, my thoughtful ways, the rhythm of my voice, and my family's special traditions. • As an African American, I have a history to be proud of and a culture to celebrate. It's up to me to learn as much as I can about the struggles and victories of my people. I can talk to grown-ups about the past. I can watch documentaries and read books about the great things African Americans have done. • It wasn't always so easy to learn about ourselves. That's why Carter G. Woodson, the noted African

American historian, started Negro History Week in 1927. He wanted people everywhere to know about the historical and cultural contributions of Black people in America. • We now celebrate Black History Month because of Mr. Woodson's desire that we all know and be proud of our rich and colorful past.

FEBRUARY 1

It's an honor and a privilege to
be Black.

FEBRUARY 2

Today I will feel special, not
because it's Black History Month,
but because I am Black all the time.

FEBRUARY 3

America is my homeland. I am
proud of the wonderful history
of African Americans, and I
promise to pass it on.

FEBRUARY 4

I will always stand up for my right
to be me.

FEBRUARY 5

Science, music, business, and art. I
can pick any field and find a great
Black achiever who's made his or
her mark.

FEBRUARY 6

In the faces of Black people I see strength and pride.

FEBRUARY 7

Africa is the motherland, the continent of my ancestors. I will study the history of Africa.

FEBRUARY 8

I am a proud child of African descent.

FEBRUARY 9

I look in the mirror. I see my textured hair, my full lips, my dark skin. These are the beautiful gifts of my ancestors.

FEBRUARY 10

I am a chocolate-colored child. That's one of the reasons I'm so sweet.

FEBRUARY 11

I will learn about the culture of Black
people who live all over the world, in
places like Europe, Brazil, and
Trinidad.

FEBRUARY 12

Bessie Coleman had to go all the way
to Europe to learn how to fly
a plane. She became the first Black
lady pilot. I want to be a pioneer, too.

FEBRUARY 13

There are heroes all around me. I see heroes every day in my family, friends, and neighbors.

FEBRUARY 14

Today I'll let the world know who I am. I'm an African American and I am proud of it.

FEBRUARY 15
My heritage is as beautiful and as
colorful as a hand-stitched quilt.

FEBRUARY 16
Dark and strong like the soil of the
earth, that's me.

FEBRUARY 17

Catfish, collard greens, and sweet
potato pie. These are foods to feed
our bodies and our spirits. That's
why they're called "soul food."

FEBRUARY 18
I celebrate Black History every day.

FEBRUARY 19
George Washington Carver thought
of more than three hundred things
to make from the peanut. Professor
Carver saw endless possibilities
in a little peanut. I see endless
possibilities within myself.

FEBRUARY 20

Red stands for the struggles of
my people. Black represents the
richness of our skin. Green is for
the land of Africa. These are the
colors of our African American flag.

FEBRUARY 21

I'll ask my parents and grandparents
to share their stories of the past. I
will learn what Black people went
through to bring me to today.

FEBRUARY 22

Today I will learn six facts about a famous African American.

FEBRUARY 23

My ancestors fought for my freedom. I will remember this. I am grateful.

F E B R U A R Y   2 4

Jazz, blues, gospel, and rap music
are forms of storytelling rooted in
my African past. I will listen closely.

F E B R U A R Y   2 5

When I look to the sky, I see the
same stars that led slaves to
freedom. I'm stargazing at our past.

FEBRUARY 26
Madam C. J. Walker was a successful
businesswoman and inventor who
made her own line of hair-care products.
Today I can start a business of my own.

FEBRUARY 27
Black *is* the perfect color for my skin.

FEBRUARY 28
I am the hope for the future, born to do
great things.

March

M Y   F A M I L Y

My family is made up of people whom I love and people who love me! We love and respect one another, just the way we are. • Families come in all kinds, but the love of a family always stays the same. We fuss, disagree, and sometimes we just don't get along, but we continue to love and support each other. • Our family's love is like a warm blanket we all get under together. We eat together, live together, and solve our problems together. • Jazz trumpeter Wynton Marsalis comes from a family in which some of the boys are musicians. His brothers Branford, Delfeayo, and Jason each has his own musical talent. Although these brothers play different instruments they are still part of the Marsalis family.

March 1
Listen up, family! I'm so glad
you're mine.

March 2
Everyone's family is different.
Some families have fathers and
mothers, some have brothers or
sisters, some have grandpas or
grandmas. Families are just
different people loving, living,
and working together.

MARCH 3

Of all the things that I love, I love
my family best.

MARCH 4

Today I will remember all the nice
things my family does for me. I'm
lucky to have my family.

MARCH 5

My parents teach me the things
I need to know when I grow up.
I thank my parents for always
teaching me.

MARCH 6

Traditions like a Friday-night fish
fry and a secret recipe for tea
cakes help make my family unique.

MARCH 7

How do I treat the grown-ups in my family? I am polite and respectful at all times.

MARCH 8

When I look at our family photo album, I see Mama as a little girl and Gramps with hair and no glasses. I'm looking at our family history.

MARCH 9

No matter what I may do, the
people who care about me love
me all of the time.

MARCH 10

Sometimes I'm right, sometimes
I'm wrong. Sometimes we fight,
sometimes we get along. But we
always love each other. We're a
family.

MARCH 11

Today I will think of a wonderful
surprise that I can do for my father
or mother, brother or sister.

MARCH 12

I am not afraid to ask for help from
my family when I need it.

MARCH 13

When I feel scared, I'll tell
someone who cares about me.
I am safe and protected in the
arms of my family.

MARCH 14

In my family love doesn't run out.
There is always plenty of love to
go around.

MARCH 15

At family reunions I get many
special gifts: the smell of Uncle's
famous barbecue, dancing with
cousins, and Auntie's pinches on
the cheek. I also get to know my
family tree. Today I will ask Mom
and Dad if I can help plan a family
reunion.

MARCH 16

Whenever I have a big problem, I'll talk about it with someone who loves me. By sharing my problem I give a bit of it away.

MARCH 17

Today I will ask Mom or Dad to spend some time with me. I'll let them know that our time together is my best time of day.

MARCH 18

Whenever I see something that needs to be cleaned up at home, I won't worry about who made the mess. I'll just clean it up.

MARCH 19

Home is where my family is, and that's where I belong.

MARCH 20

I love my parents, and my parents
love me. We have a special circle
of love.

MARCH 21

I tell people in my family what
I want and what I need. I let
them know what I am feeling.

MARCH 22

Today I will cheer up a relative who lives alone. I'll call them just to say, "Hey."

MARCH 23

I am a member of a team called FAMILY.

MARCH 24

When I need some attention, I can ask to spend time alone with my mom or dad.

MARCH 25

Mealtime is a time for sharing stories, telling jokes, and talking about our day. It's our get-together time, and I love it.

MARCH 26

Today I will tell someone in my family what I love about them most. Maybe they'll share what they love most about me.

MARCH 27

In my family there is love. I am loved. I am loving toward others.

MARCH 28

Today I will give the people in my
family a little gift. I can give them
a hug, a smile, or maybe just ten
minutes of peace!

MARCH 29

My parents don't always use
words to tell me they love me.
They tell me with all of the things
they do for me.

MARCH 30

Being a mom or dad must be a hard job. Today I'll try and make it a little easier. I'll do what my parents ask me to do, with no fussing.

MARCH 31

Today I will rise, and shine my love on everyone in my family.

April

F A I T H

*F*aith is a force that comes from inside me. Faith helps me to believe in the power of God, in myself and what I can do. It's a trust that things will always turn out all right. • I have faith in God and the miracles God can perform. I see proof of God's work every day in the beautiful colors of the earth, in the flowers, a sunset, cloud patterns, and people. • When Ben S. Carson was in fifth grade, he was having trouble in math, not reading well, and getting bad grades. Ben's mother insisted that Ben and his brother do well in school. Because Ben's mother believed in him, he began to believe in himself and his abilities. • Ben discovered that he loved learning new things, and he started to do very well in school. He attended Yale University and the University of Michigan Medical School. He is now a pediatric neurosurgeon. • Whenever I think I can't achieve my goals, I'll remember that Dr. Ben Carson had to struggle at first, but he had faith in himself, and he succeeded.

God holds the whole world in his hands. I am in God's loving care.

A P R I L   2

I am a gift from God, beautifully
wrapped in the colors of the earth.

A P R I L   3

Good things are happening all
around me. Thank you, God, for
each new day.

A P R I L   4

I am free to be me. I thank God
for this.

APRIL 5

I wonder what God is like. Maybe
he wears dreadlocks or likes to eat
cornbread, just like me.

APRIL 6

My God is a loving God, who gives
me everything I need.

APRIL 7

God is all good.

APRIL 8

Today I will talk with my parents
about the many ways God helps us.

APRIL 9

My day looks really good.

APRIL 10

Some days seem harder than
others, but with the power of God
I can do anything.

APRIL 11

A bird's sweet morning song. A
baby's soft smooth skin. The scent
of a flower. I notice God's handiwork
everywhere.

APRIL 12

I am a perfect child of God.

APRIL 13

When I wake up, I say, "Good morning!" I trust that today will be a good one.

APRIL 14

God has faith in me and trusts me to do what is right.

A P R I L   1 5
There is a little light inside me,
warming everyone I meet.

A P R I L   1 6
I am a brown angel.

A P R I L   1 7
No matter how things look, I know
that God is watching over me and
keeping me safe.

APRIL 18

When I pray, God hears me.

APRIL 19

God loves me.

APRIL 20

When I have to do something that is hard for me, I imagine myself doing it just right. I *can* do it.

APRIL 21

I know that everything is going to be all right. I have faith.

APRIL 22

Each day is a new day and a
chance to start over. I praise God
for this new day.

APRIL 23

Today I give thanks for each and
every gift God gives me.

APRIL 24

Even while I'm sleeping, God is
with me, giving me sweet dreams.

APRIL 25

When I'm scared, I close my eyes
and feel God's warm, loving hug.

APRIL 26

God is everywhere and is with me
all of the time. I am never alone.

APRIL 27

I am living proof of God's love!

APRIL 28

Whatever I give away always come
back to me. So I think I'll give
away love, love, love.

A P R I L   2 9

Do I have good manners? Yes, I say
"Please" and "Thank you, God."

A P R I L   3 0

Every day God just keeps on
blessing me.

May

RESPONSIBILITY

*R*esponsibility is a big word that means there are some things I am in charge of. It means knowing the difference between doing what's right and doing what's wrong. • I am in charge of what I decide to do. The way I think, the way I talk, and the way I act are all up to me. • Responsibility also means that there are some things I have to do for myself. When I clean my room, finish my homework, and do my chores, I am taking charge of the things that are mine. I can always ask for help, though, because part of being responsible is knowing that sometimes I'll need the help of others, and sometimes I'll have to give help to others. • People like Marian Wright Edelman have dedicated their lives to helping others. Ms. Edelman took on the responsibility of fighting for the rights of poor people and children. In 1973 she founded the Children's Defense Fund to work on improving the quality of life of all children now and in the future. Thank you, Marian Wright Edelman, for taking charge of keeping kids like me healthy and happy.

M A Y 1

Every morning when I wake up, I
decide what kind of person I'm
going to be.

M A Y 2

My body is precious. If I feed it
well and give it plenty of rest, it
will last me a lifetime.

M A Y 3

I brush my teeth and I wash my
face, and I even remember to wash
behind my ears. I'm neat, clean,
and looking good.

M A Y 4

My clothes are in the closet and
my bed is made. Surprise! I'm
keeping my room clean, and
tomorrow I'll do it all over again.

M A Y 5

Today I will make a special card
for my mom and dad. I'm sending
love notes.

M A Y 6

Mama folds the clothes, Papa cuts the grass, and I dust the furniture. We're a family working together every day.

M A Y 7

I take care of my sisters and brothers, I play games with them, or maybe I just keep them company. I am dependable.

M A Y   8

Sometimes the older people in my
family need help getting around;
sometimes the younger ones do, too.
I'm happy to help whoever needs it.

M A Y   9

Grandmother used to take care of
Mom when Mom was little. Now I
help Mom take care of Grandmother.
That's three generations of love
and care.

MAY 10

Homework, doing chores, and having fun are kids' business. Kids' business is my business.

MAY 11

Books, pencils, paper, and a smile. I bring my materials and a learning attitude to school.

MAY 12

I love and respect all books. They
are my friends, and I treat them
kindly.

MAY 13

When I play with my friends, I play fair. I take turns and I never hit someone else.

MAY 14

Every day I'll think about what I'm going to say before I say it. The words I speak can be helpful or hurtful. I respect the power of my words.

M A Y   1 5

I have a loud voice I use outside
and a soft voice I use inside. I
know how to use my voice
properly.

M A Y   1 6

Having a library card is an
important privilege. When I check
out books, I read and take care of
them and return them on time. I
always return what I borrow.

M AY 1 7

Rules are to keep me safe. That's why I obey rules.

M AY 1 8

After a day of playing, I put my toys away. Then I'll know where to find them.

M AY 1 9

I am proud of my neighborhood; I put trash where it belongs.

M A Y   2 0

Taking part in student government
elections is good practice for
voting when I'm older. I want my
vote to count.

M A Y   2 1

I can be trusted to make the right
decisions. Drugs and alcohol are
not for me.

M A Y   2 2

I recycle bottles, cans, and
newspapers. I am doing what I
can to protect the Earth.

M A Y   2 3

Today I will set a good example.
You never know who is watching.

MAY 24

When something is bothering me,
I'll change only the things that I can.
I'll change my mind, my attitude,
and my actions.

MAY 25

Do I listen closely when other people
are talking? From now on, I'll give
them my full attention.

MAY 26

It's not always my fault when things go wrong. Sometimes mistakes happen.

MAY 27

I don't need to make up stories. It's so much easier to tell the truth.

MAY 28

Church is a sacred place. I respect it. It fills my heart with peace and love.

MAY 29

I'm happy for the talents that God has given me. They are special gifts, and it is my responsibility to use them.

MAY 30

Animals love good, fresh water and a clean place to stay. I take good care of my pets every day.

MAY 31

I take excellent care of all the treasures I have—my books, my pets, my family, my toys, and myself.

June

My feelings are always changing. They get hurt, they get happy, they get angry, and sometimes they just get totally out of control! That's why I have to remind myself that feelings come and go like the wind.

• Sometimes I wish I were an actor like Whoopi Goldberg; then I'd have a written script to tell me what to say and how to act. Whoopi Goldberg began acting on stage when she was eight years old. She went on to star on Broadway, host her own talk show, and win an Academy Award. • It's Whoopi's job to make her audience know exactly what her character is feeling. I guess it's my job to let those around me know exactly what *I'm* feeling.

J U N E   1

I don't worry about what other
people think of me. I am not
afraid to be different.

J U N E   2

My feelings are not good or bad,
they just are.

JUNE 3

Sometimes I can choose my
feelings. I can choose to laugh,
not cry. I can choose to be calm,
not angry. I can choose to be
happy, not sad.

JUNE 4

I am patient. I can wait as long as
I have to.

June 5

Just for today, I don't whine, cry, or pout when things aren't going my way.

June 6

Being angry makes me want to scream, shout, and stomp. I'll count to ten instead. Whew, I feel better now.

JUNE 7

I can admit when I've made a mistake. I'm brave enough to say when I'm wrong.

JUNE 8

When I get tired and cranky, I can take a nap or go to bed for the night. Soon I'll be rested and ready.

June 9

I promise to accept one thing
about myself that I don't like,
because God made me perfect.

June 10

I am a good kid.

June 11

Today I will find a quiet spot. I'll
have some quiet time, just for me.

JUNE 12

I know that it's good to cry
sometimes. Crying washes away
the hurt.

June 13

I'm not afraid to say I'm sorry, especially when I hurt someone's feelings.

June 14

Hey, bad feelings, sad feelings, get out of here! I've had enough of you.

J U N E 1 5

When I get mixed up, I clear away
my thoughts and I give my brain a
new start.

J U N E 1 6

When something inside of me
says, "I can't do this," I'll quickly
kick that negative voice away. I
have no doubts that I *can*.

JUNE 17

I know it really doesn't help to worry about my troubles. It *does* help to talk things over with someone else.

JUNE 18

I can let go of old stuff—old grudges, old hurts, and old attitudes.

JUNE 19

I like surprises—special treats that
let me know someone is thinking
about me.

JUNE 20
Here comes that tingly feeling in my tummy, and before I know it, I'm cracking up!

JUNE 21
I have so many chores to do. After I'm done, I'm gonna take a kids' break—thirty minutes of downtime.

JUNE 22

I can say no to things that don't
feel right to me.

JUNE 23

Sometimes I do my best to solve a
problem, and it just doesn't work.
There is nothing wrong with
asking for help.

J U N E   2 4

When the people I love have to go
away, I'll remember that sad
good-byes will turn into happy
hellos when my loved ones return.

J U N E   2 5

Today I will remember the face,
voice, and smile of someone who
is no longer with me.

J U N E   2 6

My curiosity is a good thing.
That's why I ask lots of questions.

JUNE 27

One of the hardest things about growing up is new feelings and changing bodies. But I can handle these things.

JUNE 28

When kids are mean to me, I know that I am not the problem.

JUNE 29

Sometimes I wake up laughing, I
go through the day goofy, I come
home silly, and I go to sleep
tickled. I've had a good day.

JUNE 30

God's world is full of magic. When
I watch a bird take off and fly with
a flap of its wings, I'm amazed.

July

IMAGINATION

I love the world of pretend, where I can take off for grand adventures in another time or place. • With my imagination, I can also see things in my mind the way I want them to be—me doing a perfect dive or winning the spelling bee. • The next step is believing in myself and using my energy to make my dreams real.

That's what Augusta Savage did when she refused to give up on her dream to be a sculptress. Against her father's wishes and despite being poor, Augusta found a way to study art in New York and France. • Her talent was noticed, and Ms. Savage was hired to sculpt a bust of W. E .B. Du Bois and to create a special sculpture for the 1939 New York World's Fair.

JULY 1

My imagination is a very special gift. It can take me anywhere I want to go.

JULY 2

I'm full of ideas.

July 3

Great things often start with a
dream in somebody's head. When
I'm willing to do some work, my
dreams can come true.

July 4

When I grow up, I might be a
nurse, a writer, or a firefighter.
Whatever I decide to be, I'm sure
I'll be good at what I do.

J U L Y 5

Today I will take my thoughts
someplace fun and exciting. Maybe
I'll sneak into a candy factory or
stow away on a pirate ship.

J U L Y 6

I am as colorful as a butterfly, and
I am just as free to fly.

JULY 7

Fish chewing bubble gum, dogs
driving cars, and giraffes on
skateboards. It's amazing to me
the things my mind can think up.

J u l y 8

I see a world where everyone gets along. Love is in our hearts and peace is our favorite song. It's a perfect world.

J u l y 9

Using my imagination I can go anywhere I want to go, be what I want to be, and do all that I want to do.

JULY 10
If I use my head, I can always
make something out of nothing.

JULY 11
I can build cardboard houses
and make tin-can cars. I can
design spaceships that fly me
to the stars. My imagination is
a wonderful tool.

JULY 12

Daydreaming is my first step to reaching for the stars.

July 13

My mind is a big pot filled to the
rim with scary stories, folktales,
and knock-knock jokes. My mind
is always cooking up something good.

July 14

Today I'll pretend I'm living back in
the good old days. No television, no
cars, and no video games. There's just
lots of time to talk, play, and read. I
could get to like this.

J U L Y   1 5

I will look at my old toys and think
of ways to turn them into new toys.

J U L Y   1 6

Lights! Camera! Action! My favorite
movie is on, and I'm playing the
leading role.

JULY 17

My mind sees the picture, my
hands do the work. I'm making a
masterpiece.

JULY 18

There's nobody else like me in the
whole wide world. *Imagine that.*

J U L Y   1 9

I'm going to travel in my mind,
maybe somewhere faraway or
maybe just around the corner. I'm
going places.

J U L Y   2 0

Today I'll pretend that I'm a fighter
pilot like the famous Tuskegee
Airmen. Look at me, I can fly.

J U L Y   2 1

I always have new hopes and
dreams for my future.

J U L Y   2 2

Elementary school . . . junior high
. . . high school . . . college. My
future begins one step at a time.

J U L Y   2 3

When I imagine being kind, I *am*
kind.

J u l y   2 4

Today I will imagine ways to help others.

J u l y   2 5

In my imagination the skies are green, the trees are blue, and the water is purple. I am coloring my world.

July 26

When I'm outside I can be a loud, fierce lion. I can roar and hear the playful sound of my voice. I'm the mighty king of the jungle.

July 27

I think my dreams are God's way of showing me the things I can be.

July 28

I don't think I'll try to grow up too fast. I'm going to enjoy being a kid.

July 29
When I rest my eyes, I peek at all
the treasures in my mind.

July 30
With my imagination I can make
wishes come true.

July 31
Today I am an explorer. I'm off to
see what new things I can discover
in my own backyard.

August

J O Y

*J*oy comes from the people and the things that I love. It's that wonderful feeling that bubbles up when I'm outside playing and I see Daddy walking home from work. It's being so happy when my best friend gets to spend the night. • Joy is the sound of music filling my house as we dance and sing along with Stevie Wonder. An award-winning singer and composer, Stevie Wonder had his first number one hit when he was just twelve years old. His happy, hopeful songs about love, peace, and growing up always make me feel good. They remind me that the greatest joy comes from inside.

August 1

The sun is shining. I'm shouting,
running, skipping, and jumping
for joy.

August 2

I'm full of God's energy.

August 3

My happiness starts on the inside
and ends up on the outside.

AUGUST 4

Today I'll smile. My sunny smile
tells it all.

AUGUST 5

When I spread joy to others, it
comes back to me.

AUGUST 6
I am happy and thankful for
everything I have.

AUGUST 7
There's magic in Grandmother's
arms. Her soft skin and sweet
voice warm me like a blanket
of love.

AUGUST 8

I am full of God's grace. That's
true joy.

AUGUST 9

Sometimes life tickles me and I just
have to laugh out loud.

AUGUST 10

Today is a great day. I won't let
anybody take away my joy.

AUGUST 11

At least once a day I'll treat myself
to all the nice places in my mind.

AUGUST 12

Today I will find joy in small things—a sandwich that I make myself, my mother's hug, the gentle touch of a kitten.

AUGUST 13
Laughter makes a happy mind and heart.

AUGUST 14
I can act silly. I can blow bubbles. I can do somersaults in the grass. Being a kid is fun.

AUGUST 15
I like sharing God's joy with others.

AUGUST 16

Today I'm going to have myself a
mighty good time, no matter what
the day brings.

AUGUST 17

I am a magnet for fun and friends.
Good things always find their way
to me.

A U G U S T   1 8

Joy is my daddy's hello hug or my
mommy's good-night kiss. Joy is
the love in my family.

A U G U S T   1 9

I say words that are helpful, kind,
and true, so that others can hear a
little bit of joy, too.

August 20

I make sure that when others meet
me they go away feeling good. I
always try to be polite.

August 21

Today is my day to have fun.
Whether I'm chasing my brother
or playing dress-up with my sister,
I love being a kid.

A U G U S T   2 2
My heart and my life are full of joy
and love.

A U G U S T   2 3
Joy is that really good feeling I get
when I do something nice for
someone else.

A U G U S T   2 4
I always see the good in everyone.

AUGUST 25

A candy bar, a dog's wet nose, or
a simple thank-you; I like small
joys, too.

AUGUST 26

My smile can turn into a snicker,
then a laugh that goes on and on.

AUGUST 27

Today I will think of happy
memories that make me smile.

AUGUST 28

When I'm feeling down, I can try
to fill my mind with good, happy,
funny thoughts.

AUGUST 29

I am beautiful to see.

August 30

Yes, indeed, I feel wonderful, I look fabulous, and I am going to have a most spectacular day.

August 31

Today is a day that the Lord made for me to use and enjoy.

September

SCHOOL

School is a wonderful place to spend my time. It's where I learn math, explore science, and read about adventures. • Learning is something that never stops, even after I'm grown-up. I will come to school every day prepared and ready. I'll pretend that I am a sponge sitting at my desk soaking up all the knowledge that my teacher has to share. • There is a school in Chicago called Westside Prep that was started in 1975 by Marva Collins with just eighteen students. Marva decided to teach students that weren't doing their very best at their regular schools. Marva now has over two hundred students in her school. I like to think that Marva helped turn her students into learning sponges, too.

SEPTEMBER 1

Outstanding. That's the word I use to describe myself and my schoolwork.

SEPTEMBER 2

Sometimes I make mistakes, but it's okay. Mistakes are chances for me to learn.

SEPTEMBER 3

Today I will learn the meaning of one new word. I will use it in a sentence at least three times during the day.

SEPTEMBER 4

Whatever it is I need to do, I'll jump right in and lend a hand.

SEPTEMBER 5

School is the right place for me to show off how clever, curious, and bright I am.

SEPTEMBER 6

Listening is the key to learning. I'm listening and learning every day.

SEPTEMBER 7
School is a place to learn and
grow, full of facts, friends, and fun.
I love my school.

SEPTEMBER 8
At school my teachers are there to
teach me, and I am there to learn.

SEPTEMBER 9
I will ask my teacher for help
when I need it.

SEPTEMBER 10

Today I will challenge myself by reading something new, maybe a book about ancient Africa or the great pyramids of Egypt.

SEPTEMBER 11

I watch the world around me, and learn from the actions of others.

SEPTEMBER 12
In everything I do, I do the very best I can.

SEPTEMBER 13
The best way to learn something that's difficult is to do it over and over. After a while, it'll get easier.

SEPTEMBER 14

When my teacher gives me a test,
I don't need to worry. I've studied
hard, I've studied right, and I'm
ready.

SEPTEMBER 15

I can write a story about me,
about you, about anything.

SEPTEMBER 16

When I finish studying and doing
my chores, I'll take a break and
read a book for fun.

My way isn't the only way of
doing things. I will listen and learn
from others.

SEPTEMBER 18

I learn something new every day. I love learning new things.

SEPTEMBER 19

After school, doing my homework always comes first.

SEPTEMBER 20

After a hard day at school I take time to stretch, relax, and just chill.

SEPTEMBER 21
The world is a large place and I want to see it all.

SEPTEMBER 22
I am an excellent reader, understanding every word, every sentence.

SEPTEMBER 23
Today I'll make an extra effort to listen carefully to my teacher.

SEPTEMBER 24

The key to mathematics is figuring out the number pattern . . . the rhythm . . . the beat.

SEPTEMBER 25

When I have a question in class, I always raise my hand.

SEPTEMBER 26
I'm happy to teach others what I know.

SEPTEMBER 27
Today I prepare for tomorrow by preparing for today. I'm getting ready for my future.

SEPTEMBER 28
When I open a book, I open the door to grand adventures.

SEPTEMBER 29

If I study hard and work to do my
best, I can be whatever I want to
be when I grow up.

SEPTEMBER 30

Today my eyes are open to
discovering new things.

October

F R I E N D S H I P

*F*riends are people who share with me. It's always important to treat my friends the way I want to be treated. Swinging, playing hop-scotch, double-dutch, and tag are the fun times I enjoy with my friends. We study together and learn together. My mom says that you are judged by the company you keep, so I try and pick good friends.

• Nicholas Ashford and Valerie Simpson, known as Ashford & Simpson, are famous musicians who are married and best friends. Not only do they sing together, they write and produce their songs together. They even own a restaurant and have a radio talk show together. What an amazing and special friendship they have.

OCTOBER 1

Friends can be boys or girls, short or tall, young or old.

OCTOBER 2

I have a rainbow of friends. They come in all different colors.

OCTOBER 3

My friends don't have to look like me or dress like me or think like me. I have my own style, and my friends have theirs.

OCTOBER 4

If I borrow things from my friends I always give them back in good condition. I respect my friends and their belongings.

OCTOBER 5

I am me. You are you. That is a
wonderful thing.

OCTOBER 6

I like my friends for who they are
and how they treat me.

OCTOBER 7

The best way to have a good friend
is to be a good friend.

Today my friends and I will find
creative ways to have some fun.

OCTOBER 9

Writing letters is a good way to stay in touch with friends. I am a good pen pal.

OCTOBER 10

My friends always include me in their games. They don't care about how well I play. True friends care about how good I feel.

OCTOBER 11

When new kids move into the
neighborhood, I'll introduce myself
and show them around.

OCTOBER 12

Friends watch out for friends. If my
friends are doing something wrong
or something that might get them
in trouble, I'll speak up.

OCTOBER 13

Church friends. Neighborhood friends. School friends. Old and new friends. I have friends everywhere.

OCTOBER 14

If *your* friends play with *my* friends, then we'll all have more friends.

OCTOBER 15

One for me, one for you. Two for me, and two for you. I like giving and sharing with my friends.

OCTOBER 16

My friends and I grin and giggle, tickle and tease, and laugh for no reason at all. It's fun to be silly with my friends.

OCTOBER 17

Today I will take a moment to put myself in someone else's shoes. I'll think about what my friends need and how they feel.

OCTOBER 18

I promise to treat my friends the way I want to be treated.

OCTOBER 19

I am not afraid or embarrassed to
say I'm sorry, especially to a friend.

OCTOBER 20

Today at recess my friends and I take
turns and stand in line, without
cutting in front of each other.

OCTOBER 21

I respect my friends, and my friends
respect me.

OCTOBER 22

I just don't worry about what
other kids think or say about me,
because I happen to think I'm
pretty cool.

OCTOBER 23

Playing is not fun when someone
is getting hurt. I will listen when
my friends say stop.

OCTOBER 24

When I give away something to my friends, it no longer belongs to me. I give freely.

OCTOBER 25

I keep my hands to myself; there's nothing that anyone can say or do to me that is a reason to hit or hurt them back.

OCTOBER 26

I like it when friends tickle my ear
with little secrets. My friends can
trust me not to share the funny
things we whisper to each other.

OCTOBER 27

Is there someone in my class who
needs a friend? Today I'll be nice
to someone who may be looking
for a friendly face.

OCTOBER 28

Friends don't always have to be
people. I can always find a friend
in a book.

OCTOBER 29

My mother, my father, my sister,
my brother—these are my friends
for life.

OCTOBER 30

A true friend likes me all of the
time, just the way I am.

OCTOBER 31

When I treat myself well, I can
turn around and treat my
friends well.

November

Courage is a strong word. Having courage means I can meet any challenge. I can raise my hand in class when I have a question, go out for the basketball team, and try different styles of clothing suited just for me. • In 1960 there was a little girl named Ruby Bridges who had a lot of courage. When Ruby was only six years old, she was the first African American student to attend an all-white elementary school in New Orleans, Louisiana. All but one teacher refused to teach her. • Ruby was escorted to school every day by U.S. marshals through screaming mobs of angry people shouting hateful things. If Ruby was brave enough to do that, then I can be brave enough to face just about anything.

November 1

I have the courage to try new
things, like food from another
culture, a different hairstyle, or
a sport I've never played before.

NOVEMBER 2

Courage means not giving up even
when I'm scared. Today I'll keep
going when I want to turn back.

NOVEMBER 3

Take a good look at me. I'm
holding my head up, straight and
proud. There's no doubt about it,
I believe in myself.

November 4

When other kids are teasing or making fun of someone else, I don't join in. I have the courage to follow my own heart.

NOVEMBER 5

No putting it off, no fooling around, I'm just going to go ahead and do it.

NOVEMBER 6

I replace my friends who say "I can't" with those who say "I can."

NOVEMBER 7

I speak up for what I believe.

NOVEMBER 8

My heart and mind are strong.
I have lots of courage.

NOVEMBER 9

When something is hard for me,
I don't quit. I keep on trying.

NOVEMBER 10

My big problems can be solved a
little bit at a time.

NOVEMBER 11

God is in my life watching over
me. I am safe and protected.

NOVEMBER 12

I have the power inside of me to
face any challenge.

NOVEMBER 13

I take one step at a time, and
before I know it, I'm where I want
to be.

NOVEMBER 14

When someone is bugging me, I
just don't pay them any attention.
I'm keeping my peace.

NOVEMBER 15

If I'm called upon to speak in front of my class, I won't be afraid. I've got the facts, I speak well, and I know what I'm talking about.

NOVEMBER 16

There are many different ways to do things. You show me your way and I'll show you my way. It takes courage to see all sides.

NOVEMBER 17

I don't always like or understand
the things that happen around me,
but I can trust in God and the
people who love me.

NOVEMBER 18

I am persistent—I don't give up.

NOVEMBER 19

If a friend hurts my feelings, I'll
gather the courage to tell them
quietly and calmly.

NOVEMBER 20

I don't have to do what everyone
else is doing. I have the courage to
do what I think is right.

NOVEMBER 21

When I have a problem, I'll think of
three different ways to work it out.

NOVEMBER 22

It really doesn't matter what someone says to me. It *does* matter how I feel about it and what I choose to do about it.

NOVEMBER 23

Today I won't rush in. I'll stop and think about doing the right thing.

NOVEMBER 24

Yes! I know I can, and I won't stop
until I do.

NOVEMBER 25

A positive spirit is within me and
keeps me full of love and hope.

NOVEMBER 26

My mind is made up. Today is
going to be a great day.

NOVEMBER 27
I am always prepared with prayer.

NOVEMBER 28
I am not afraid of people, places, or things.

NOVEMBER 29
When it comes to my family and friends, I am brave enough to stand up for them.

NOVEMBER 30

With courage and determination,
Black people have lived through
many hard times. I am proud of
our history. I am proud of our
people.

December

CELEBRATION

*C*elebrations are opportunities to create memories that never leave us, memories that warm our souls when we need them. In this holiday season, I'll enjoy good food, good conversation, and good music. • During December we celebrate Christmas and Kwanzaa. Christmas is a whirlwind of colors, yummy food, and endless activities. Kwanzaa is an African American holiday that began in 1966. It starts on December 26 and ends on January 1. On each day of Kwanzaa we celebrate a different principle. • The seven Kwanzaa principles are rooted in African traditions. Each principle's name comes from the East African language of Swahili. The Kwanzaa principles are *Umoja* (unity),

Kujichagulia (self-determination), *Ujima* (collective work and responsibility), *Ujamaa* (cooperative economics), *Nia* (purpose), *Kuumba* (creativity), and *Imani* (faith). It's a time to celebrate with family and friends by acknowledging our African heritage and by renewing our faith in ourselves.

DECEMBER 1

My life is full of the promise of
new beginnings, new experiences,
and new adventures; I am ready
to begin.

DECEMBER 2

Where in the world do I want to
go? With a book and a globe, I
have my passport to go absolutely
anywhere.

DECEMBER 3

Jambo is the Swahili word for hello.
Today I will say *jambo* to everyone
I meet. It's fun learning and saying
African words.

DECEMBER 4

I feed my mind with knowledge,
my heart with love, and my spirit
with adventure.

D E C E M B E R 5

I can climb inside a book and
become a character. I'm pretending
to be someone else.

D E C E M B E R 6

There's something special about a
grandparent's love. It's that nice,
warm kind of love, the love that's
always there when I need it. I bet
my grandparents think my love is
special, too.

DECEMBER 7

Cookies in the oven. A friend's surprise visit. A letter in the mail for me. Good things happen to me all the time.

DECEMBER 8

It's the holiday season, and joy is spreading all around.

DECEMBER 9

I say a prayer for peace, and I ask that it start with me.

DECEMBER 10

Today I will learn about Kwanzaa, the only original African American holiday, which is about two weeks away.

DECEMBER 11

What's there to snack on? Grapes, cheese, and trail mix.

DECEMBER 12

I respect myself, my family, and my home at all times.

DECEMBER 13

Today I'll start a family tradition. How about a concert with home-made instruments?

DECEMBER 14

What do I smell coming from the kitchen? It's something yummy. I'll get my apron, because I'm ready to help.

DECEMBER 15

When God speaks to my heart, I listen.

DECEMBER 16

I notice and respect the talents of others. I tell them how gifted they are.

DECEMBER 17

The holiday season is for families.
We laugh, tell stories, and catch
up on old news.

DECEMBER 18

The best prayer of all is a simple
prayer of thanks. Thank you, God.

DECEMBER 19

I am God's gift to the world, and
love is my gift to God.

DECEMBER 20

We're sending holiday cards with a picture of me inside. Here's my love to you.

DECEMBER 21

Today I'll remember that *love* is the heart of Christmas.

DECEMBER 22

When caroling, or baking cookies, I am sharing the holiday spirit.

DECEMBER 23
When I get dressed up and go out,
I will be on my best behavior.

DECEMBER 24
It's Christmas Eve! Let's celebrate!

DECEMBER 25
God gave me this splendid
Christmas Day to enjoy.

December 26

It's the first day Kwanzaa. We start each day of Kwanzaa by saying, *"Habari gani?"* a Swahili greeting that means, "What is the news?" For this day of Kwanzaa we celebrate *Umoja* (unity). I love working together in my family.

D ECEMBER 27

Habari gani? *Kujichagulia* (self-determination). I am in charge of my destiny.

D ECEMBER 28

Habari gani? *Ujima* (collective work and responsibility). I'll do what I can to take care of my community.

D ECEMBER 29

Habari gani? *Ujamaa* (cooperative economics). I will ask to go shopping at a Black-owned store.

DECEMBER 30
Habari gani? *Nia* (purpose). I am working on a plan to succeed.

DECEMBER 31
Habari gani? *Kuumba* (creativity). This year I will make someone a unique gift with my own two hands. *Imani* (faith). I believe in my family and in my own abilities.

INDEX

Anita Alexander and Susan Payne are co-owners of Shades of Sienna, an African American children's bookstore in Oakland, California, where they live. This is their first book.

Illustrator Nancy Doniger's work has been widely published in the *New York Times*. She is the illustrator of several books for children, including *Morning, Noon, and Night: Poems to Fill Your Day* compiled by Sharon Taberski. Ms. Doniger lives in Brooklyn, New York.